LADYBIRDS

designed and written by Althea
illustrated by Barbara McGirr

Longman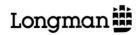

Spring is here.
Ladybirds wake up from
their long winter sleep and
fly off in search of food.

Ladybirds' hard wing cases protect
their delicate wings.
Ladybirds taste nasty.
They are brightly coloured
to warn birds not to eat them.

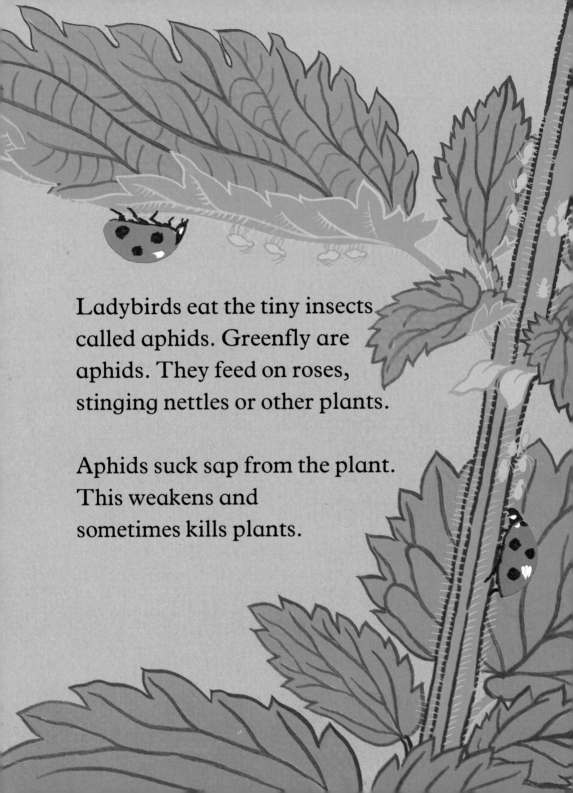

Ladybirds eat the tiny insects
called aphids. Greenfly are
aphids. They feed on roses,
stinging nettles or other plants.

Aphids suck sap from the plant.
This weakens and
sometimes kills plants.

A male and a female ladybird mate.
The female lays her eggs
on the plants where
the aphids are feeding.

The eggs are sticky so they don't fall off.
She will lay about 500 eggs
which takes her ten days.

The eggs darken.
After a few days the larva struggles
out of its egg to search for aphids.
It feeds by sticking its hollow
jaws into an aphid and
sucking out the juices.

Large aphids try to escape by
kicking away the larva or
squirting sticky liquid
on the larva's head.
Aphids may also escape by
falling off the plant.

The larva, which eats several hundred
aphids, gets bigger and bigger.
Its skin keeps getting too tight.
The skin splits and the larva
wriggles out wearing a new skin.
Soon it will be ready to change
into a pupa.

The larva makes a sticky glue and
attaches its tail to a plant.
The last skin splits away
and there is the pupa
hanging from the plant.

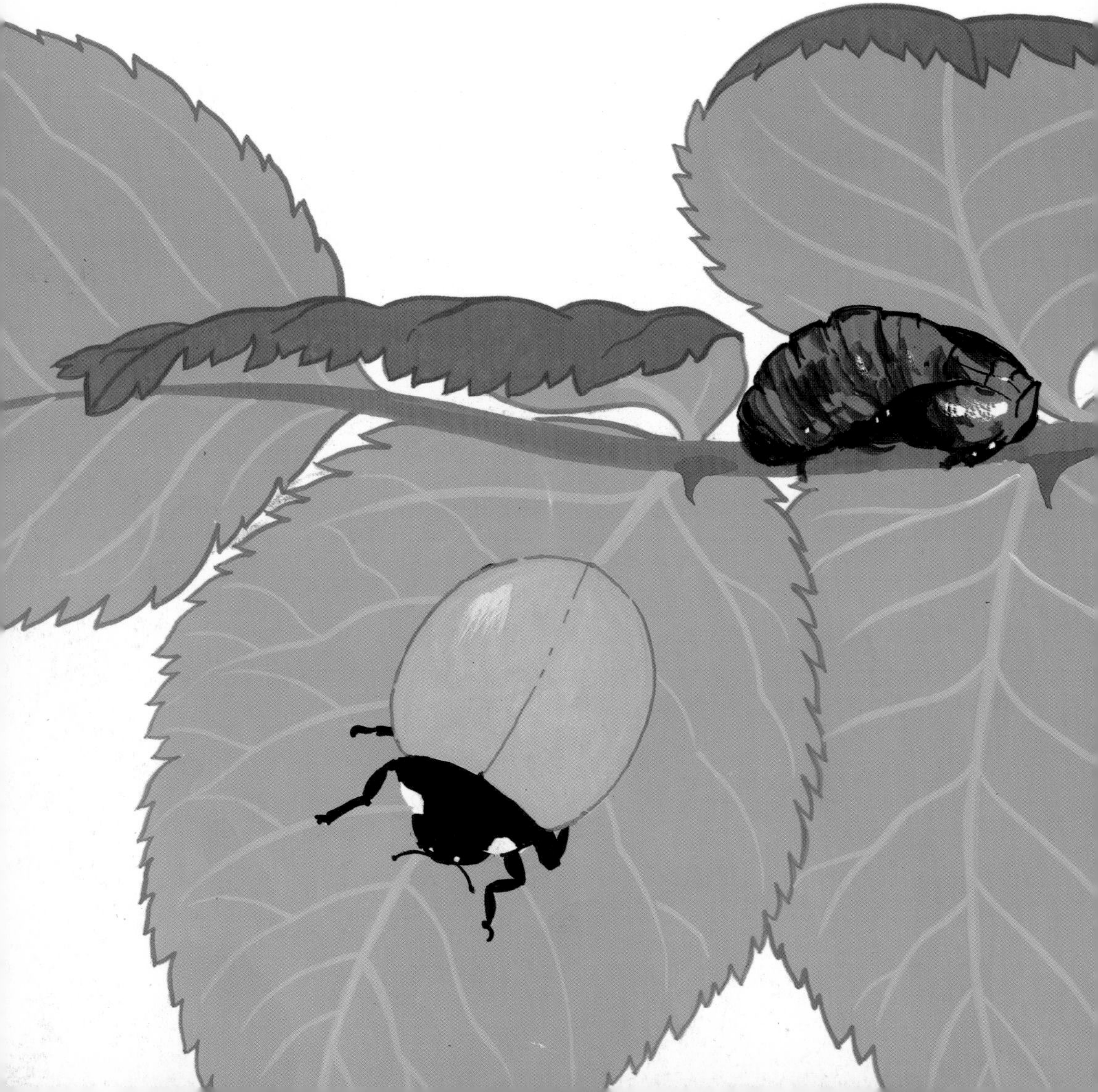

A week passes.
The pupa cracks open and an
adult ladybird pushes its way out.
It rests for a few hours while
its wing cases harden and
change colour. Then it can fly off
in search of more aphids.

Aphids will often eat too much sap and
ants feed by sucking some of this
sap from them.

The ants chase both ladybirds and
larvae away from the aphids.
In defence, ladybirds and larvae bleed a
smelly yellow liquid which the ants hate.

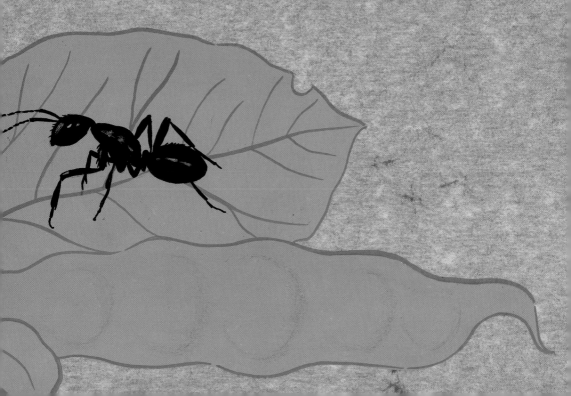

Sometimes when ladybirds are
frightened they will fall on
their backs and pretend to be dead
until the danger has passed.

As well as eating aphids, ladybirds
sip nectar from flowers.
They do not grow bigger but they
need food to give them energy
to fly and to help them live
through the winter.

When the cold weather begins
ladybirds search for safe places
to sleep for the winter.
Ladybirds often sleep together
in large groups.

In very cold winters many will die.

When Spring arrives
ladybirds wake up and
fly off in search of food.

Ladybirds help farmers and gardeners
by keeping down the numbers of aphids.
Sadly, insecticides which farmers and
gardeners use to kill insects,
often kill ladybirds too.

LONGMAN GROUP LIMITED
Longman House
Burnt Mill, Harlow, Essex CM20 2JE, England
and Associated Companies throughout the World

First published 1985

ISBN 0 582 25260 1 (pbk edition)
ISBN 0 582 25263 6 (csd edition)

Set in 'Monophoto' Plantin 18/24 pt

Produced by Longman Group (FE) Ltd
Printed in Hong Kong

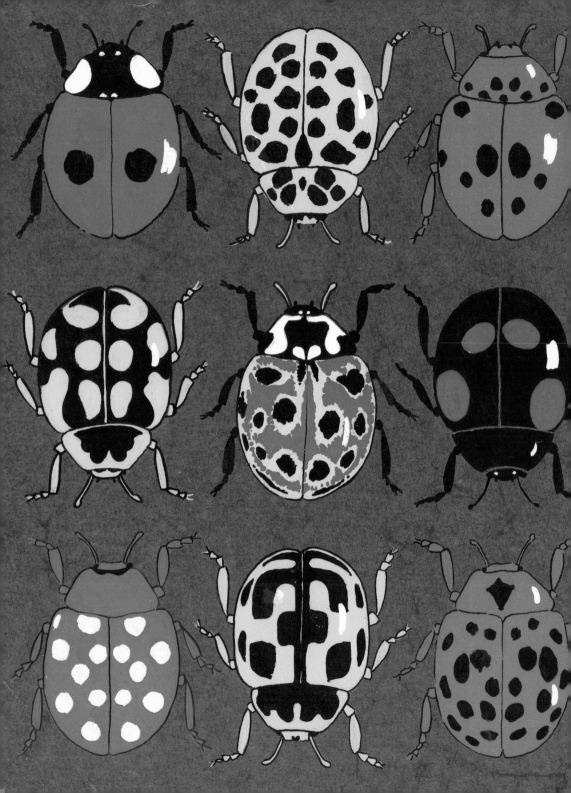